Brush With Greatness

Goya

Tamra B. Orr

PURPLE TOAD
PUBLISHING

Printing   1   2   3   4   5   6   7   8   9

Goya
Leonardo da Vinci
Michelangelo
Monet
Van Gogh

Publisher's Cataloging-in-Publication Data
Orr, Tamra.
    Goya / written by Tamra Orr.
        p. cm.
Includes bibliographic references, glossary, and index.
ISBN 9781624691911
1. Goya, Francisco, 1746-1828—Juvenile literature. 2. Artists—Spain—Biography--Juvenile literature. I. Series: Brush with greatness.
    N7113.G68 2017
    759.6

Library of Congress Control Number: 2016937167

eBook ISBN: 9781624691928

ABOUT THE AUTHOR: Tamra B. Orr is a full-time writer and author living in the Pacific Northwest. She has written more than 450 nonfiction educational books for all ages. She loves learning about the world, from exotic locations and animals to fascinating people in history. When she is not writing books, she is reading books and writing letters — or looking through art books and marveling at how artists can help you see the world in new ways.

Contents

The ancient city of Cadiz in southwest Spain is full of domes and watchtowers.

SPAIN

France

Cadiz

N

Chapter 1
Helping the King

"Go now, son," my father signed to me. His hands flew through the air, and I watched carefully so as not to miss anything. "You cannot be late. The Great Goya needs you!"

My father had been born deaf. He learned a way to talk using his hands called sign language. Mother and I learned as well. I was almost as fast as my father now.

Pulling on my shoes, I wondered what it was going to be like to be Señor Goya's assistant while he was in Cadiz. People were saying that the famous portrait painter was ill. No one knew what had made him so sick, but one thing was clear.

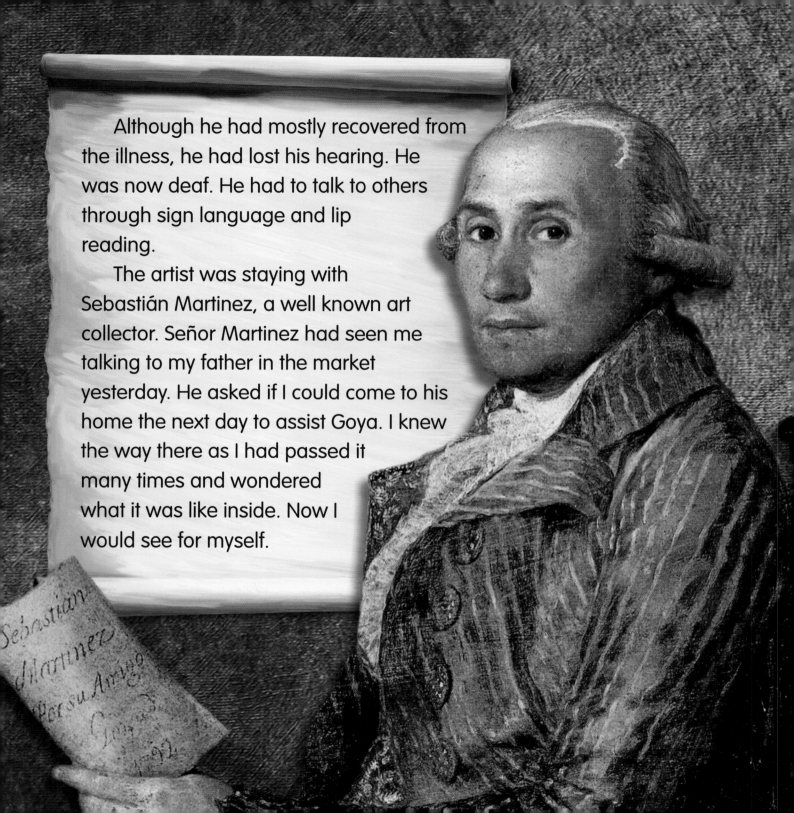

Although he had mostly recovered from the illness, he had lost his hearing. He was now deaf. He had to talk to others through sign language and lip reading.

The artist was staying with Sebastián Martinez, a well known art collector. Señor Martinez had seen me talking to my father in the market yesterday. He asked if I could come to his home the next day to assist Goya. I knew the way there as I had passed it many times and wondered what it was like inside. Now I would see for myself.

Goya often painted the people he knew best, including his host Martinez (left) and King Charles III during a hunting trip.

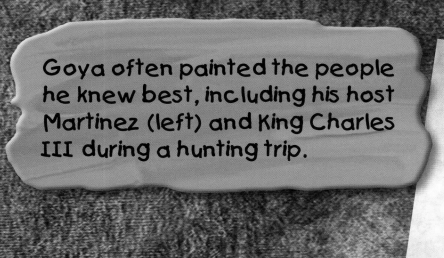

"Listen and learn today, Matteo," my father advised me before I walked out the door. "Señor Goya is the Painter to the King. It is the highest position any painter can have. So, you will be serving your king well by helping Señor Goya share his words with others."

I held my head high as I walked. I was helping the king!

Chapter 2
Meeting Goya

I tried not to show how nervous I was when Señor Martinez invited me into his fancy home. "Greetings, young Matteo. Follow me and I shall introduce you to our guest," he said.

I followed him down the hall, staring at the amazing paintings decorating each wall. When we entered the home's library, I gasped. I had never seen so many books in one place before.

"Ah, a reader," said Martinez, with a smile. He then pointed to the gentleman stretched out on the couch. "Matteo, may I present Señor Francisco José de Goya, the king's painter."

Goya's portrait of Queen Maria Luisa on her horse shows her strong personality.

Goya smiled as I stepped forward. He was a middle-aged man with brown curly hair. He had a wide mouth and broad nose. His dark eyes looked dull. It was clear he wasn't feeling well.

I signed, "It is an honor to meet you." The artist sat up straighter and his eyes brightened. He patted the couch seat next to him.

I sat down, and he began talking to me. It was a mix of sign language, odd gestures, and a few words. I paid close attention so I could follow what he was saying.

"My deafness is maddening," he explained. "I hear noises in my head, but nothing outside of it." He sighed. "Tell me of King Charles IV. What is the news?"

"He seems to be letting others run the kingdom these days. My father thinks he listens too much to Queen Maria Luisa," I replied.

Goya's face lit up. "My own thoughts exactly! She should stick to riding that horse I once painted her on. Your father sounds like a very wise man."

I nodded. Wait till my father hears that.

"Enough of this," Goya said, standing up. I quickly took his arm to steady him. "To the studio," the painter said. "I have much to show you."

Fisherman with a Rod, 1775

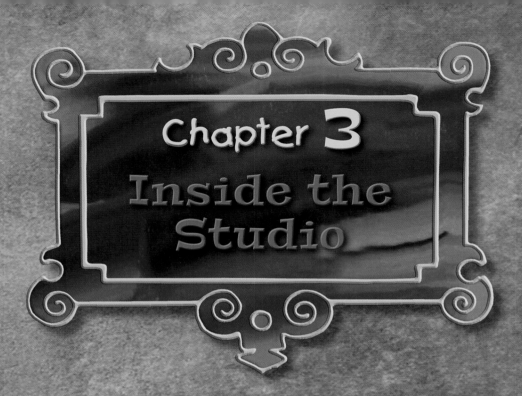

Chapter 3
Inside the Studio

Walking into the room that Goya was using for his studio, I was greeted by walls covered with beautiful paintings, sketches, and even tin plates covered in oil paint.

Goya chuckled as he explained, "I started my career by creating dozens of paintings as patterns for the royal tapestries [wall hangings]. I painted simple images like people hunting or fishing, or kids playing outside," he explained with his hands. "They are hung in the palace dining room. That is how I became King Charles' First Painter."

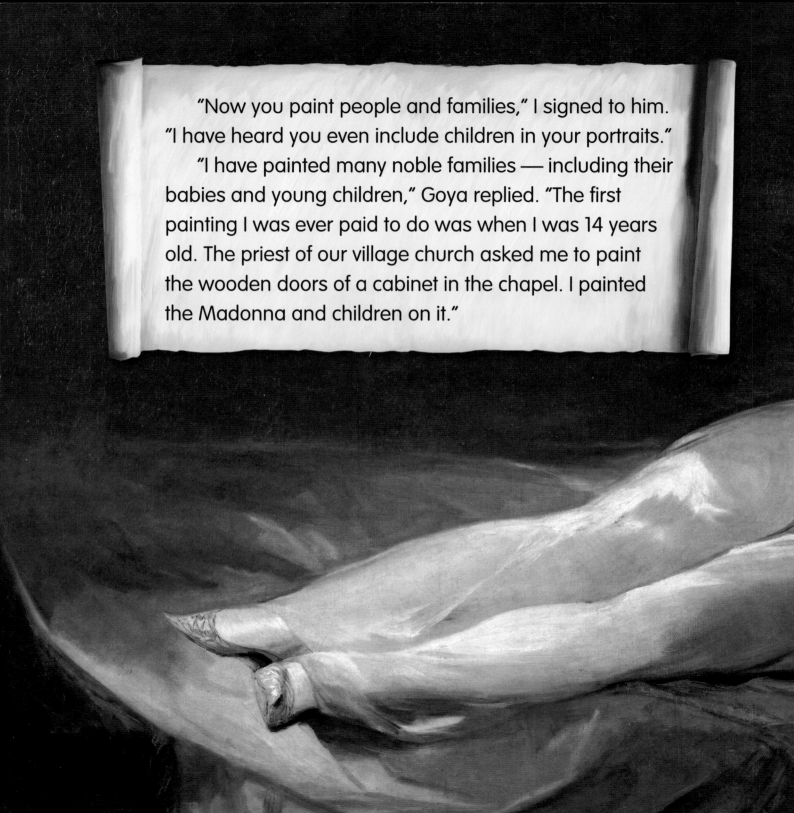

"Now you paint people and families," I signed to him. "I have heard you even include children in your portraits."

"I have painted many noble families — including their babies and young children," Goya replied. "The first painting I was ever paid to do was when I was 14 years old. The priest of our village church asked me to paint the wooden doors of a cabinet in the chapel. I painted the Madonna and children on it."

Goya painted many portraits, some with clothes (*The Clothed Maja*, 1800-1805) and some without (*The Nude Maja*, 1799–1800.)

Goya's *The Parasol was* turned into a royal tapestry.

Chapter 4
As If by Magic

"I have seen a few of your paintings, Señor Goya," I told him. "I like how you paint everyone — not just the people of nobility. I have heard you have painted card players, fruit sellers, gypsies, and even men fighting in taverns. They all seem the same to you."

Goya smiled at me. Slowly, he stood up and walked over to a blank white canvas. "Painting is about showing real life, Matteo," he said. "Let me show you how it is done."

He picked up his brush and attacked the blank canvas. He was a sloppy but passionate artist. Rags littered the floor. Flecks of paint were everywhere. In a matter of minutes, the outline of a face appeared.

Boys Picking Fruit shows how much Goya enjoyed painting children at play.

It was like magic, it happened so quickly. One minute it was just a few dark strokes of paint. The next it was a face. A moment later, it was *my* face!

For the next half hour, Goya added shadows and lines to my portrait. When he was done, I saw a young boy who looked both proud and shy.

"There you are, young man," said Goya. "We shall call it *Portrait of a Boy Who Understood the Deaf Goya*. I shall take it back to Madrid with me, as I leave in just a few weeks to attend a meeting of the Royal Academy. The king demands my return."

He added, "This portrait will serve as a reminder that, despite the loneliness and sadness I feel from my deafness, I am not alone. For that, I thank you."

Goya placed his hand on my shoulder. It was the same hand that had just held the paintbrush.

There was no need for words.

We both understood that we had found a way to help each other.

In later years, Goya's paintings began to take on darker ideas, such as *The Devil's Lamp* and *The Sleep of Reason Produces Monsters*.

Chapter 5
Unforgettable

Through the years, I had often heard news about the deaf artist. Soon after we parted, Goya created a series of eighty spooky drawings. Some of the names sounded like they came out of a Halloween story: *Witches' Flight, The Devil's Lamp,* and *The Sleep of Reason Produces Monsters*. These works showed ghosts and witches and other creepy things.

Clearly, Goya had not given up on doing portraits. He was named First Court Painter, with the job of painting nobles and their families. In *The Family of Charles IV* (1800–1801), he even painted himself at his easel behind the royal family.

Goya was known for sometimes including himself in paintings. This was very rare for painters of his time.

24

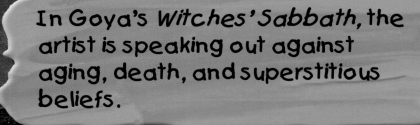

In Goya's *Witches' Sabbath*, the artist is speaking out against aging, death, and superstitious beliefs.

Goya would go on to do a series of prints called *The Disasters of War* (1810–1820) in protest of war. While his work proved his loyalty to Spain, he would never work for the royal family again.

He expressed his disappointment through his artwork. He painted another series known as the *Black Paintings*, filled with witches, beasts, and classic images from dark tales.

Finally, I heard, the famous artist had had enough. In 1824, he moved to France, where he lived out the rest of his life. He died in 1828. My great Goya was gone. Though I may sigh at this thought, I still say to myself, in the sign language we shared, "Goodbye, my friend. I will never forget you."

GOODBYE

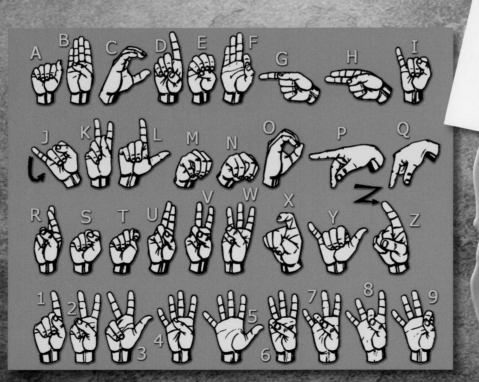

Hundreds of years later, sign language is still used to help the deaf communicate.

Timeline

1746	Francisco José de Goya y Lucientes is born on March 30 in Fuendetodos **(fwen-day-TOH-dohs)**, Spain.
1761	He is asked to create cartoons for the Royal Tapestry Factory in Madrid.
1771	He opens his own studio and is given his first assignment: to paint a decoration in a small cathedral.
1773	He marries Josefa "Pepa" Bayeu.
1775	He and his family move to Madrid to create tapestries for the Prince of Asturias (who will become Ferdinand VII).
1783	Francisco Javier is born, the only child of Goya's to survive until adulthood.
1786	Goya is named painter to King Charles III.
1789	Under Charles IV (ruled 1788–1808), Goya is promoted to court painter.
1793	An illness leaves Goya deaf. He moves in with Sebastián Martinez in Cadiz **(ka-DEEZ)**, Spain. France declares war on Spain.
1799	Goya is promoted again—to First Court Painter. He completes many portraits of nobles.
1808	Napoleon Bonaparte invades Spain; Goya pledges allegiance to Napoleon's brother, Joseph Bonaparte.
1810	He paints a portrait of Joseph Bonaparte and is awarded the Royal Order of Spain. Goya begins painting *The Disasters of War*.
1812	His wife dies.
1814	Napoleon is defeated. The Spanish king Ferdinand VII takes the throne.
1824	Goya retires to Bordeaux, France. He dies in 1828.

The Quail Shoot, 1775

Further Reading

Books

Alexander, Heather. *Child's Introduction to Art: The World's Greatest Paintings and Sculptures.* New York: Black Dog & Leventhal, 2014.

Cesar, Stanley. *Twenty-Four Francisco Goya's Paintings (Collection) for Kids.* Amazon Digital Services, 2014.

Heine, Florian. *13 Painters Children Should Know.* New York: Prestel Publishing, 2012.

McNeese, Tim. *Francisco Goya (The Great Hispanic Heritage).* New York: Chelsea House, 2008.

Rockett, Paul, and Ruth Thompson. *Francisco de Goya.* Danbury, CT: Franklin Watts, 2016.

Wood, Alix. *Francisco Goya (Artists through the Ages).* London: Windmill Books, 2013.

Works Consulted

The Best Artists, "Goya's Mysterious Illness." Word Press.com, https://100swallows.wordpress.com/2008/07/06/goyas-mystery-illness/

Carr-Gomm, Sarah. *Goya.* New York: Parkstone Press Ltd., 2005.

Centellas, Ricardo. "Info de Goya: Physical and Psychological Profile." University of Zaragoza. http://goya.unizar.es/InfoGoya/Life/Caracter.html

"Don Sebastian Martinez y Perez (1747–1800)." *Heilbrunn Timeline of Art History.* http://www.metmuseum.org/toah/works-of-art/06.289

Felisati, D., and G. Sperati. "Francisco Goya and His Illness." U.S. National Library of Medicine, National Institutes of Health; ACTA Otorhniolaryngological Italica. October 5, 2010. http://www.ncbi.nlm.nih.gov/pmc/articles/PMC3040580/

Gallaudet University, "The Abbe Charles Michel de l'Epee." Galludent University. http://giving.gallaudet.edu/HOF/pastinductees/the-abbe-charles-michel-de-lepee

Goya News: http://www.eeweems.com/goya/index.php

Heilbrunn Timeline of Art History, "Francisco de Goya (1746-1828) and the Spanish Enlightenment." The Metropolitan Museum of Art. http://www.metmuseum.org/toah/hd/goya/hd_goya.htm

Licht, Fred. *Goya.* Abbeville Press Publishers, 2001.

"A Timeline of the Life of Goya." Erik E. Weems. http://www.eeweems.com/goya/bio_timeline.html

Traynor, Robert. "The Deafness of Goya." *Hearing Health & Technology Matters,* November 27, 2012. http://hearinghealthmatters.org/hearinginternational/2012/the-deafness-of-goya-part-ii/

Waldron, Ann. *First Impressions: Francisco Goya.* Harry N. Abrams, Inc. 1992.

On the Internet

Art History and Artists: Romanticism from Ducksters http://www.ducksters.com/history/art/romanticism.php

Francisco Goya's *Manuel Osorio de Zuniga* at Garden of Praise

http://www.gardenofpraise.com/art55.htm

"Goya's *The Repentant Saint Peter*" at the Art Curator for Kids

http://artcuratorforkids.com/artwork-of-the-week-goya-repentant-saint-peter/

chapel (CHAP-ul)—A smaller room or area inside a church where people can go to worship on their own.

fresco (FRES-koh)—A style of painting on wet plaster so that it becomes part of a wall or ceiling.

Madonna (mah-DAH-nuh)—A painting or other art piece that shows Mary, the mother of Jesus.

nobility (noh-BIH-lih-tee)—The class of people who are high in a king or queen's government.

passionate (PASH-uh-nit)—Showing strong feeling.

portrait (POR-tret)—A painting of a person.

sign language (SYN LANG-widj)—A way to communicate using hand gestures instead of sound.

superstition (soo-per-STIH-shus)—Believing in luck, magic, ghosts, or spirits.

tapestry (TAP-es-tree)—A cloth in which images are woven, meant to be hung on a wall.

tavern (TAV-ern)—A restaurant that serves alcohol. Some taverns also rent rooms to travelers.

Index